T0372601

1 Student's Book with Digital Pack

Pippa and Pop

American English

Caroline Nixon & Michael Tomlinson

with Lesley Koustaff & Susan Rivers

CAMBRIDGE
UNIVERSITY PRESS

Map of the book

	VOCABULARY	LANGUAGE	SOUNDS AND LETTERS	LITERACY AND VALUE	NUMBERS	CROSS-CURRICULAR	PROJECT
Introduction Page 4							
1 My friends Page 6	Hello Pippa, Pop, Dan, Kim book, crayon, pencil	Hello. I'm (Pippa). What's this? It's a (pencil).	Distinguishing sounds	Duck's friend Be friendly	Numbers: 1, 2	Social studies: Sharing	Make Pippa and Pop masks
2 My family Page 18	brother, sister, daddy, mommy boy, girl, man, woman	She's the (mommy). He's my (brother). He's / She's a (boy).	Distinguishing sounds	The big carrot Help your family	Numbers: 3, 4	Science: How food grows	Make Kim, Dan, Sue and Matt finger puppets
3 My toys Page 30	ball, doll, teddy bear, train blue, brown, red, yellow	It's a (ball). It's (red).	Distinguishing between letters and objects	Big teddy bear, small teddy bear Celebrate differences	Recognizing patterns	Math: Big and small	Make a toy box and toys
Units 1–3 Review Pages 42–43							
4 My body Page 44	ears, eyes, mouth, nose arms, feet, hands, legs	Touch your (nose). Color the (arms).	Distinguishing between letters and numbers	Bunny's family Be kind	Recognizing patterns	Social studies: Feelings	Make a happy and sad face

	VOCABULARY	LANGUAGE	SOUNDS AND LETTERS	LITERACY AND VALUE	NUMBERS	CROSS-CURRICULAR	PROJECT
5 Food Page 56	*apples, bananas, cookies, sandwiches juice, milk, water*	*I like (apples).* *I don't like (juice).*	The letter sound *a*	*Picky Peter* Say *thank you*	Numbers: *5, 6*	Science: Identifying fruit	Make an apple tree or a banana plant
6 Animals Page 68	*cat, dog, fish, rabbit chair, table; on, under*	*Where's the (cat)? Here it is.* *It's (under) the (chair).*	The letter sound *e*	*Emma's new cat* Be kind to animals	Numbers: *7, 8*	Science: What animals need	Make a cat or a dog
Units 4–6 Review Pages 80–81							
7 Clothes Page 82	*hat, jacket, shoes, socks dress, pants, skirt, T-shirt*	*(Put on / Take off) your (hat).* *I have (a dress).*	The letter sound *i*	*Tommy's T-shirt* Be considerate	Shapes: *circle, square, triangle*	Art: Rough and smooth	Make a doll and its clothes
8 Transportation Page 94	*bike, bus, car, van drive a car, jump, ride a bike, run*	*I can see a (car).* *I can (ride a bike).*	The letter sound *o*	*The hare and the tortoise* Be careful	Numbers: *9, 10*	Science: Fast and slow	Make a steering wheel
9 The park Page 106	*bird, flower, frog, tree; green, pink butterflies, caterpillars, ladybugs, worms*	*A (green) (tree).* *What are these? They're (butterflies).*	The letter sound *u*	*Penny in the park* Take care of nature	One more	Math: Symmetry	Make a butterfly
Units 7–9 Review Pages 118–119							

Welcome

1 My friends

▶ 🎧³ **Listen to the song.**

Hello. I'm Dan.

Listen. Stick. Point. Say.

1 **Language practice:** *Hello. I'm (Pippa / Pop).*

🎧 ⁶ Listen. 👆 Point. ✏️ Color.

🎧 ⁷ Listen. Duck's friend

5

6

7

8

🎬 🎧⁸ Listen. 🔍 Find. 🖊 Color.

1

2

It's a pencil.

3

4

1 Language presentation: *What's this? It's a (pencil / crayon / book).*

▶ 🎧⁹ Listen. 📘 Match. 🎵 Sing.

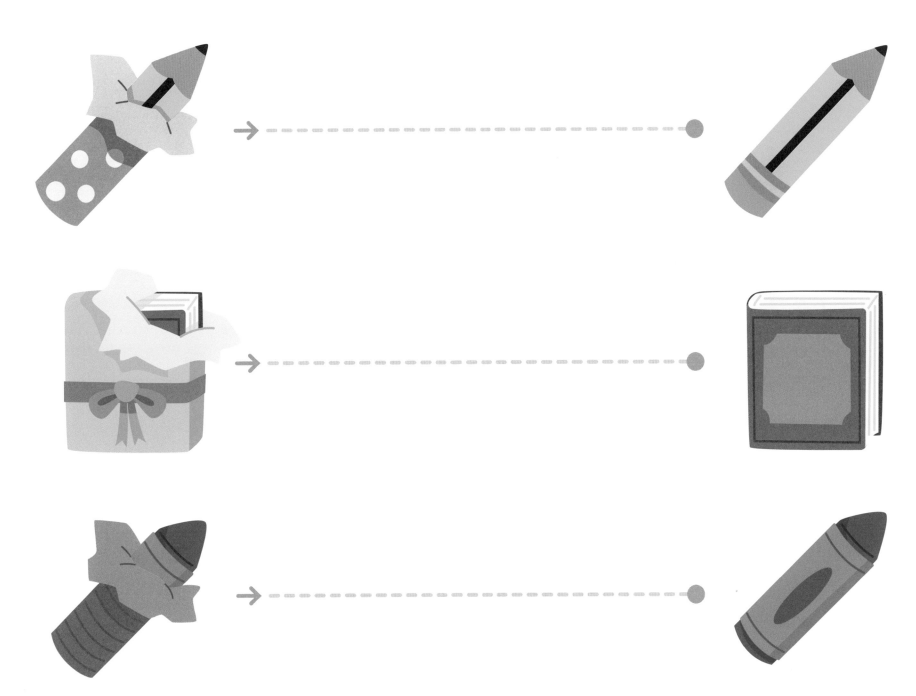

🎧 10 **Listen.** ✋ **Count.** ✏️ **Color.**

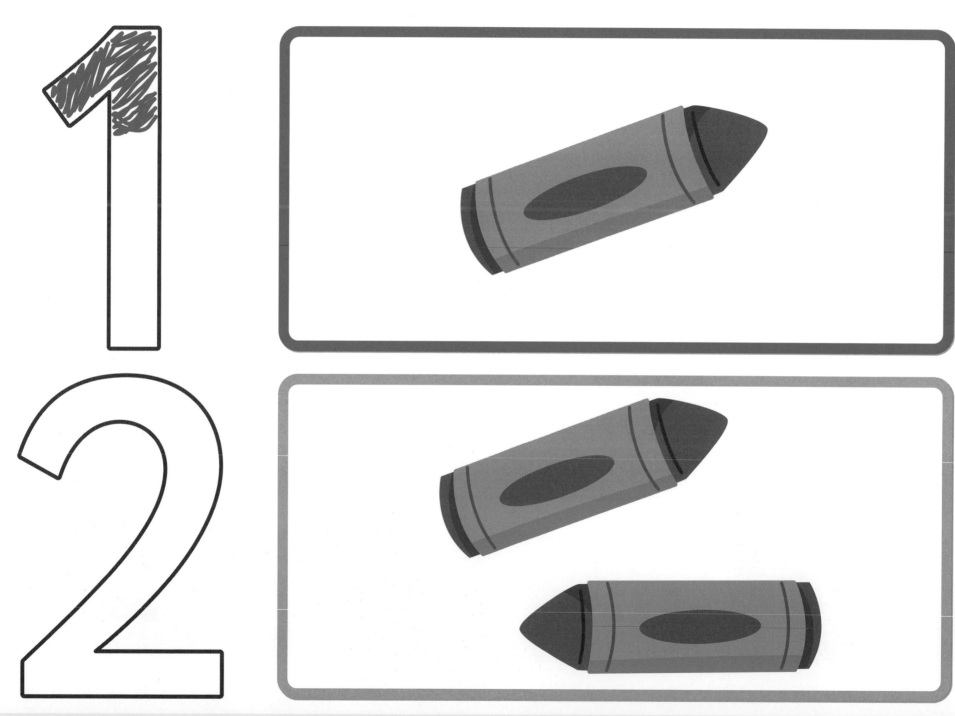

👁 Look. 📖 Match.

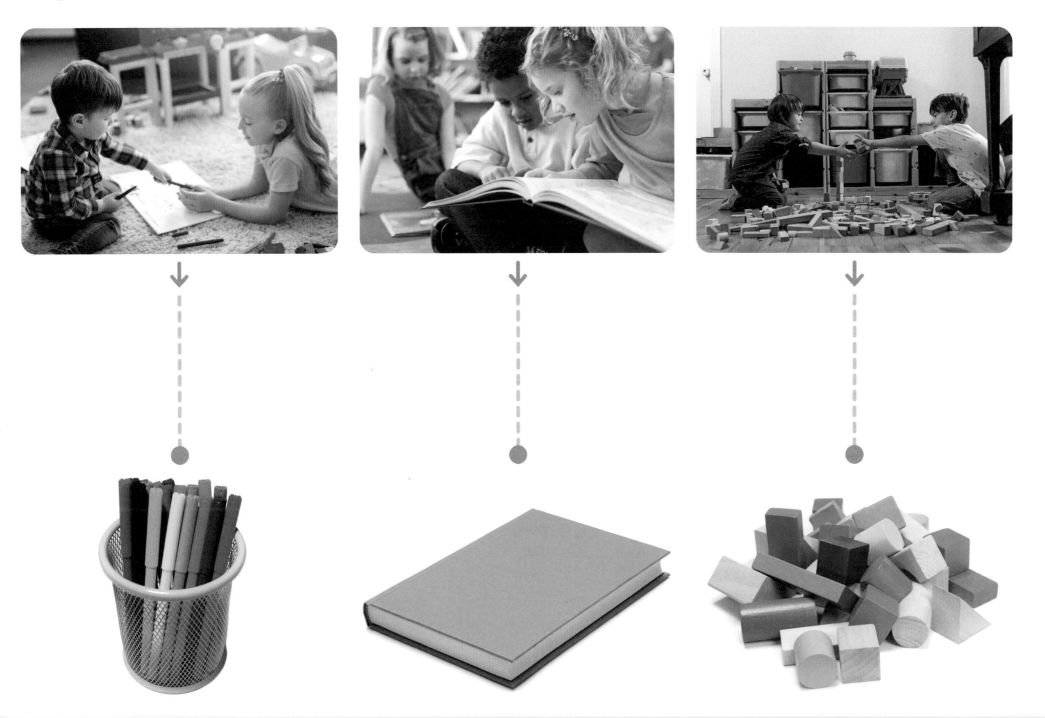

Look. **Find.** **Color.** **Say.**

1 *What's this? It's a (pencil / crayon / book).*

Look. **Make.** **Say.**

② My family

12 **Listen.** 👆 **Point.** ⭕ **Trace.**

She's the mommy.

🎧 **¹³ Listen.** ⬭ **Stick.** 👆 **Point.** 💬 **Say.**

② Language practice: *She's my (mommy / sister). He's my (daddy / brother).*

¹⁴ Listen. 👆 Point. ⭕ Trace.

He's a boy.

▶️ 🎧 ¹⁷ Listen. 📖 Match. 🎵 Sing.

🎧 ¹⁸ **Listen.** ✋ **Count.** ✏️ **Color.**

Look. Match.

Look. Find. Color the same. Say.

2 *She's a (girl / woman). He's a (boy / man).*

👁 Look. 🖐 Make. 💬 Say.

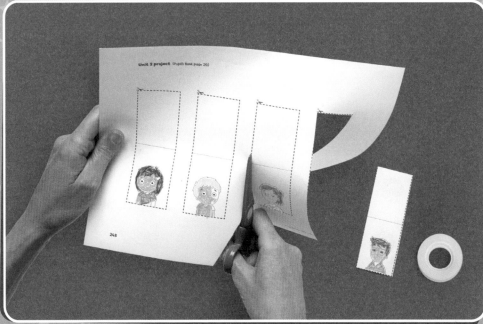

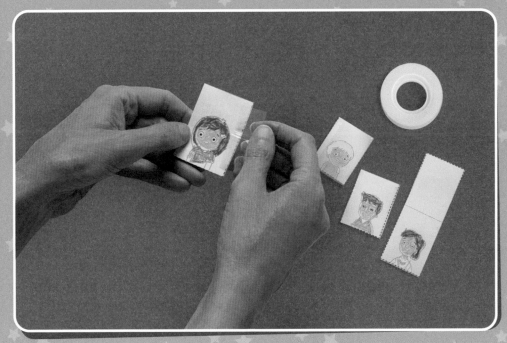

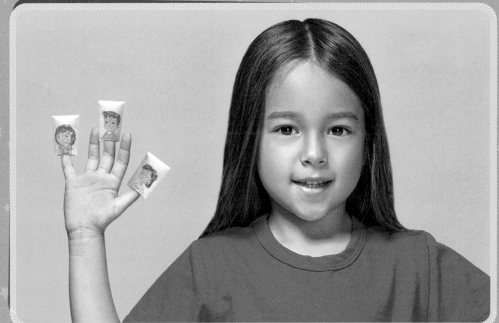

She's the (mommy / sister). He's the (daddy / brother). ② 29

3 My toys

 Listen to the song.

🎧 20 Listen. 👆 Point. ⭕ Trace.

It's a train.

🎧 ²¹ Listen. ⬭ Stick. 👆 Point. 💬 Say.

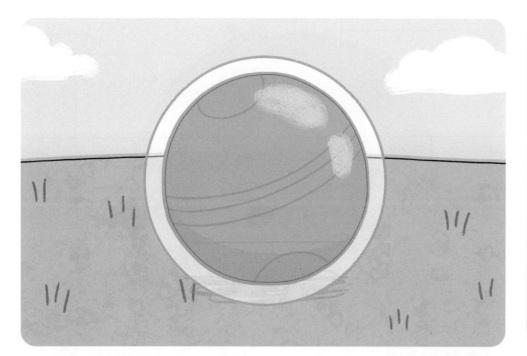

③ **Language practice:** *It's a (train / teddy bear / doll / ball).*

²² Listen. 👆 Point. ⚪ Trace.

It's red.

③ **Language presentation:** *It's (red / yellow / blue / brown).*

 **Listen.**  **Color.** 🎵 **Sing.**

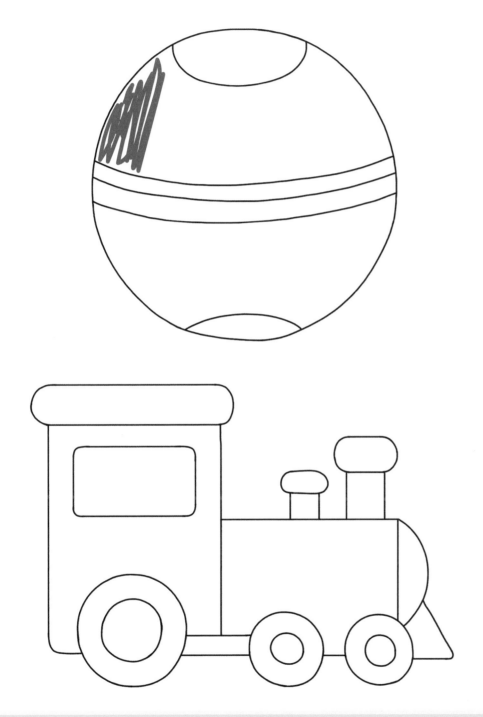

👁 **Look.** 💬 **Say.** ✏ **Color.**

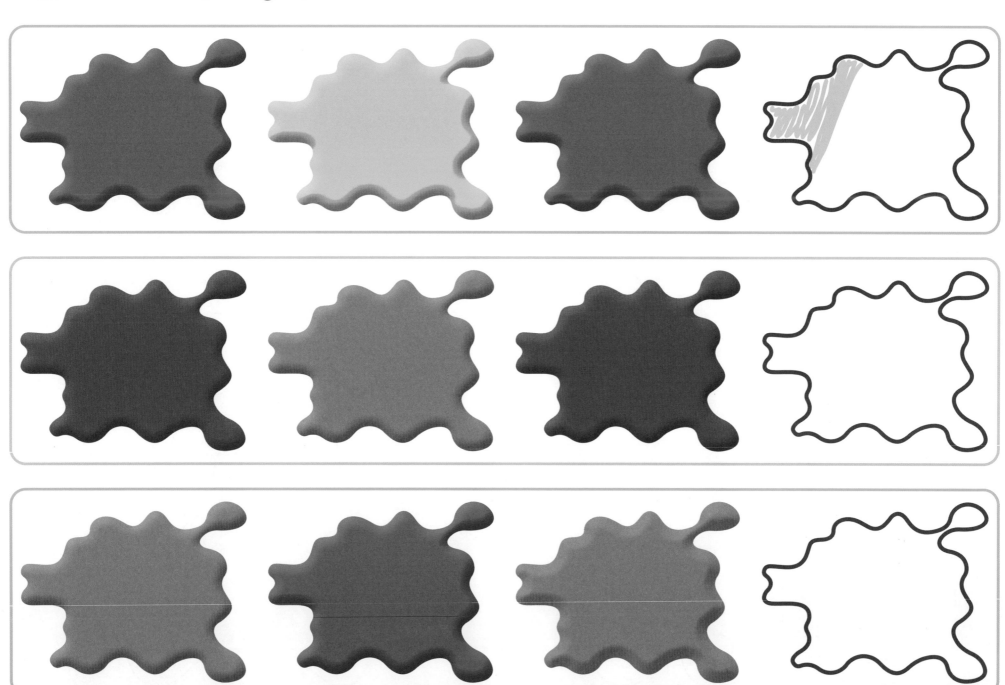

3 Recognizing patterns

👁 Look. ✏ Color.

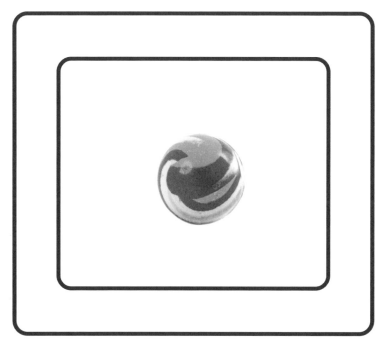

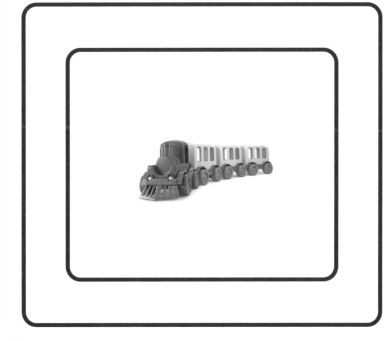

Look. **Match.** **Color.** **Say.**

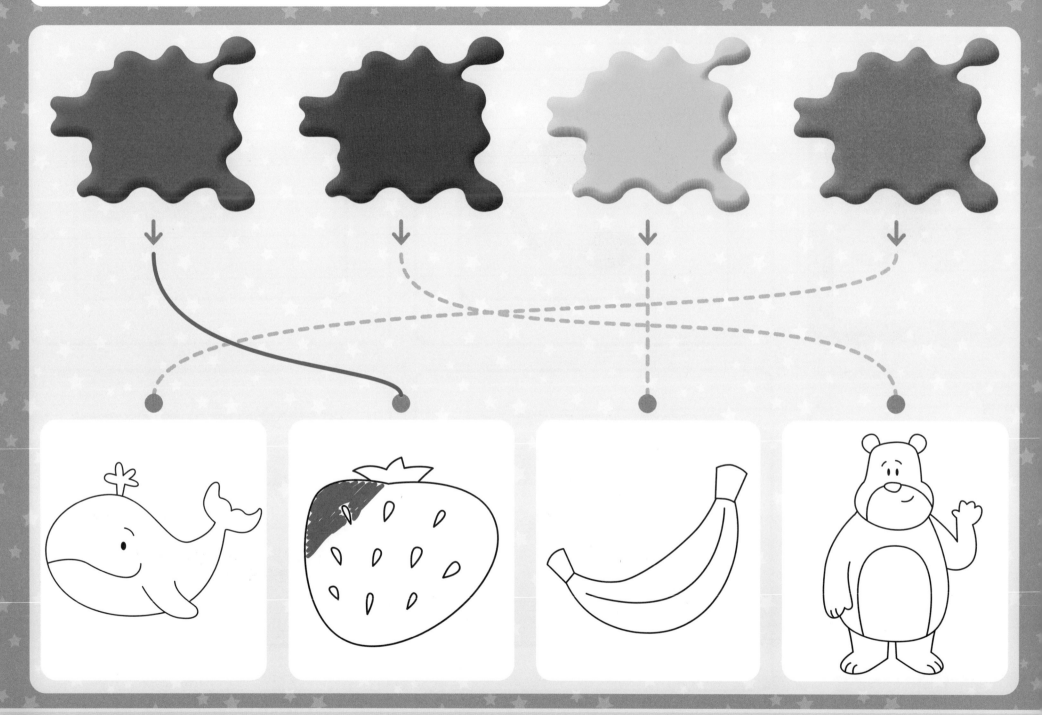

3 *It's (red / yellow / blue / brown).*

👁 Look. 🖐 Make. 💬 Say.

26 Listen. Find. Point. Say.

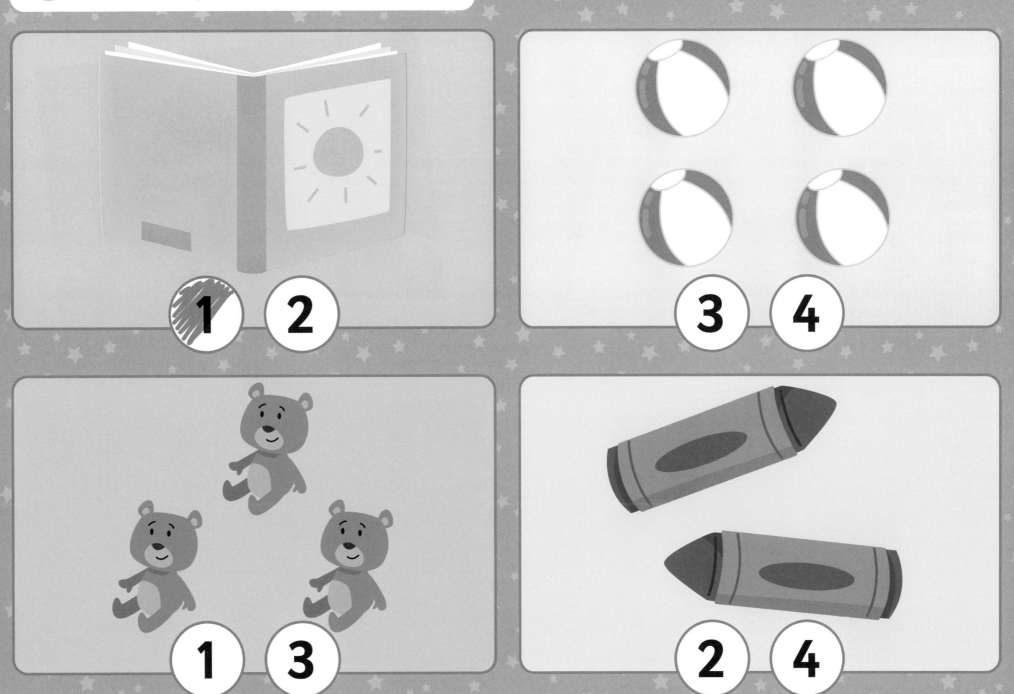

1 2

3 4

1 3

2 4

4 My body

  27 **Listen to the song.**

4 **Unit topic introduction:** Face and body

🎧 28 Listen. 👆 Point. ⭕ Trace.

Touch your mouth.

🎧 ²⁹ Listen. ⬭ Stick. 👆 Point. 💬 Say.

4 **Language practice:** *Touch your (nose / mouth / ears / eyes).*

30 **Listen.** 👆 **Point.** ⬭ **Trace.**

1

2

3

4

Color the feet brown.

 **Look.** **Match.** **Say.**

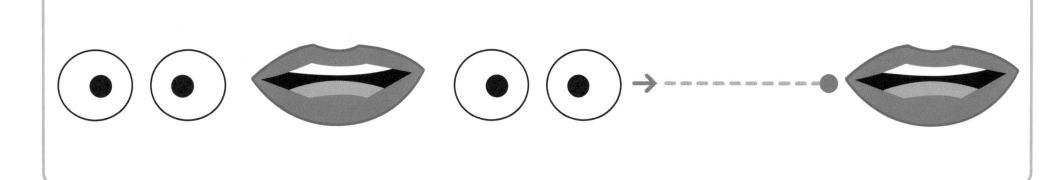

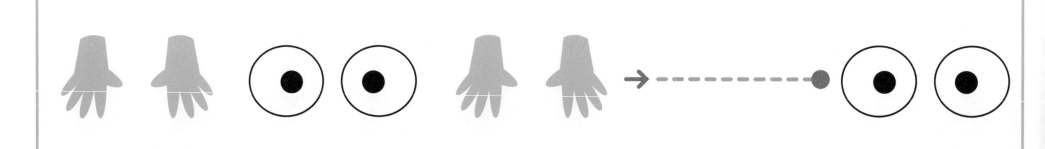

👁 Look. 🎧³⁴ Listen. ✏ Color.

🎧 **35** **Listen.** ✏️ **Color.** ✏️ **Color the same.** 💬 **Say.**

 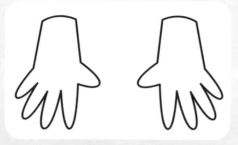  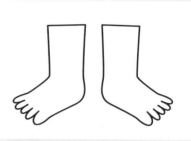

  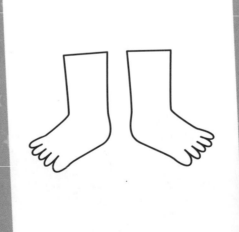 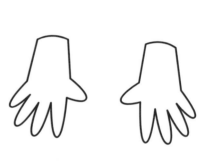

4 *Color the (arms / feet / legs / hands).*

👁 **Look.** 🤲 **Make.** 💬 **Say.**

(5) Food

  Listen to the song.

(5) **Unit topic introduction:** Food

Listen. Point. Color.

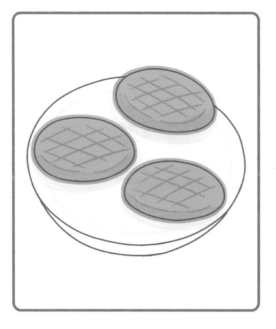

🎧 **39** **Listen.** ◯ **Trace.** ✏️ **Color.** 💬 **Say.**

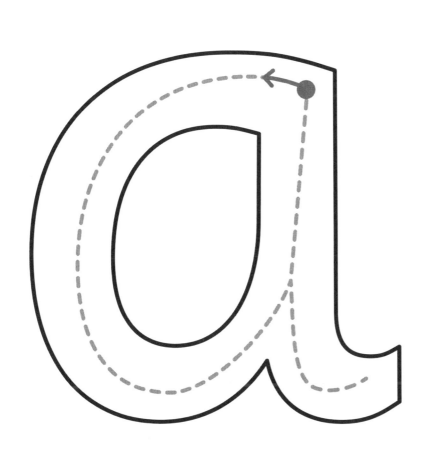

I don't like juice.

5 Language presentation: *I (like / don't like) (juice / milk / water).*

🎧 **43** **Listen.** ✋ **Count.** ✏️ **Color.**

👁 **Look.** ✏ **Color.**

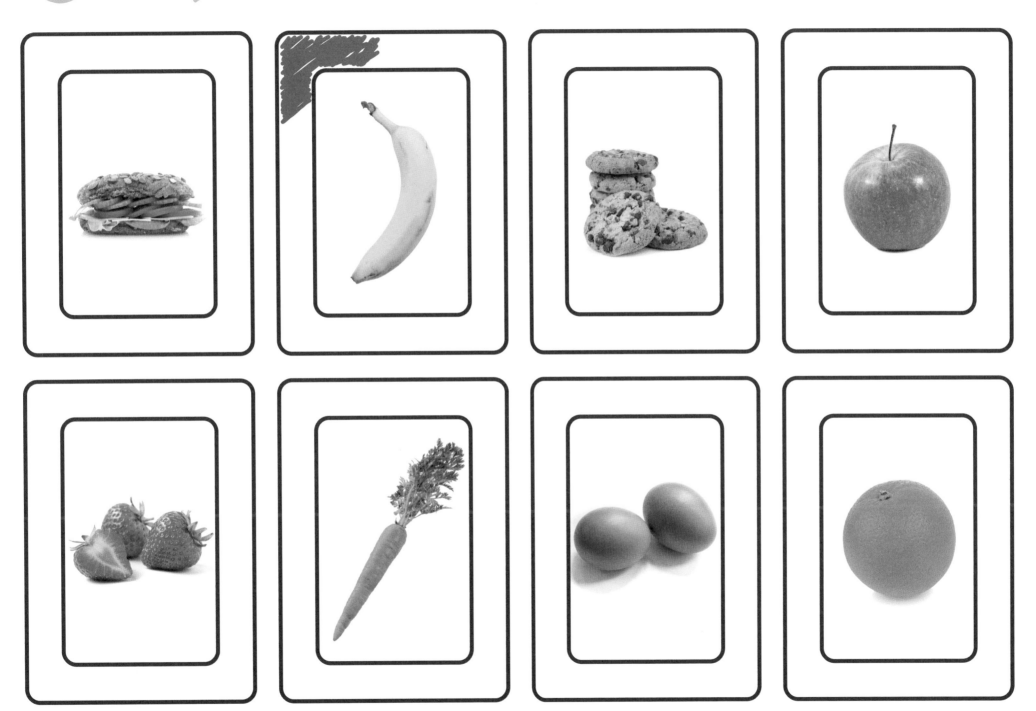

👁 Look. 🔍 Find. ✏ Color. 💬 Say.

5 *I (like / don't like) (juice / milk / water / sandwiches / cookies).*

Look. **Make.** **Say.**

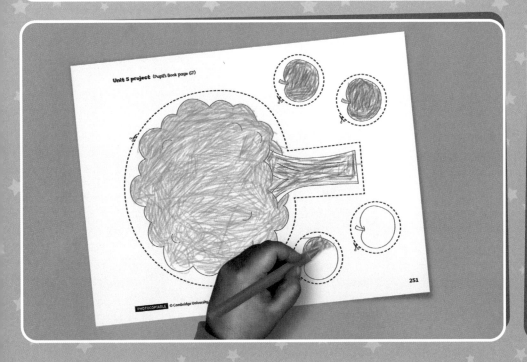

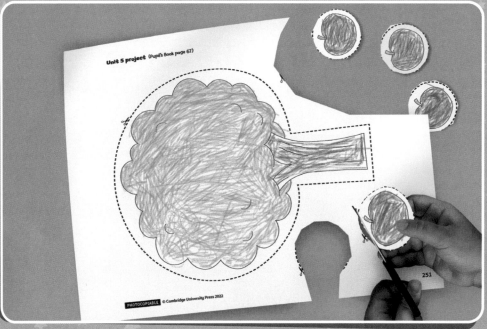

6 Animals

▶ 🎧 44 **Listen to the song.**

Where's the rabbit?

Listen. Stick. Point. Say.

6 Language practice: *Where's the (rabbit / dog / fish / cat)? Here it is.*

47 Listen. ⬭ **Trace.** ✏ **Color.** 💬 **Say.**

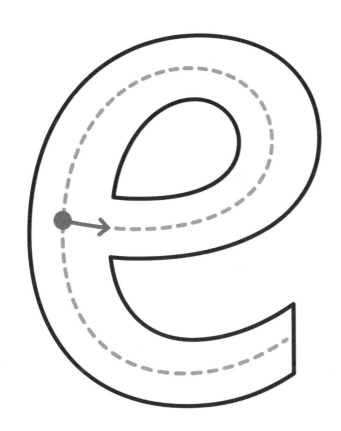

▶️ 🎧 48 **Listen.** **Emma's new cat**

6 **Language presentation:** *It's (under / on) the (table / chair).*

 **Listen.** **Color.** ♫ **Sing.**

🎧 **⁵¹ Listen.** 🖐 **Count.** ✏️ **Color.**

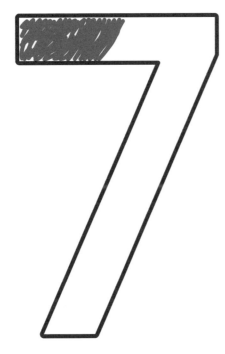

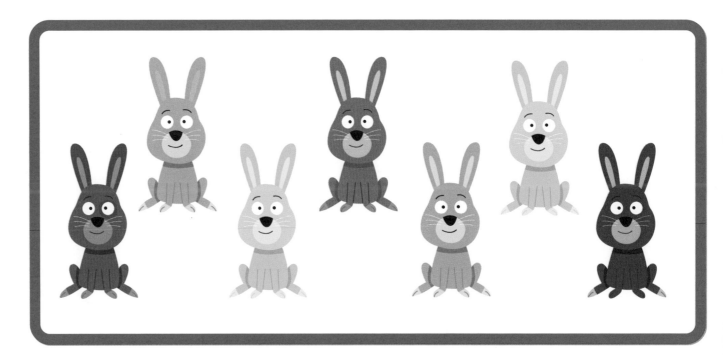

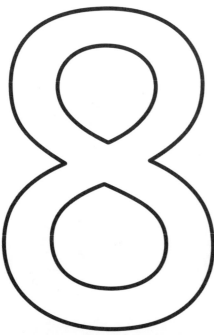

👁 **Look.** ⭕ **Trace.**

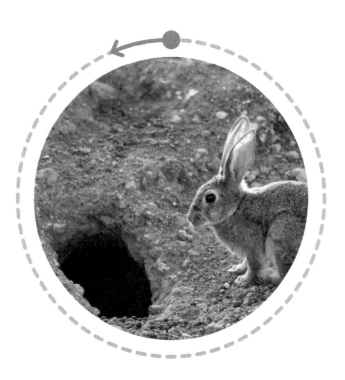

👁 Look. 📘 Match. 💬 Say.

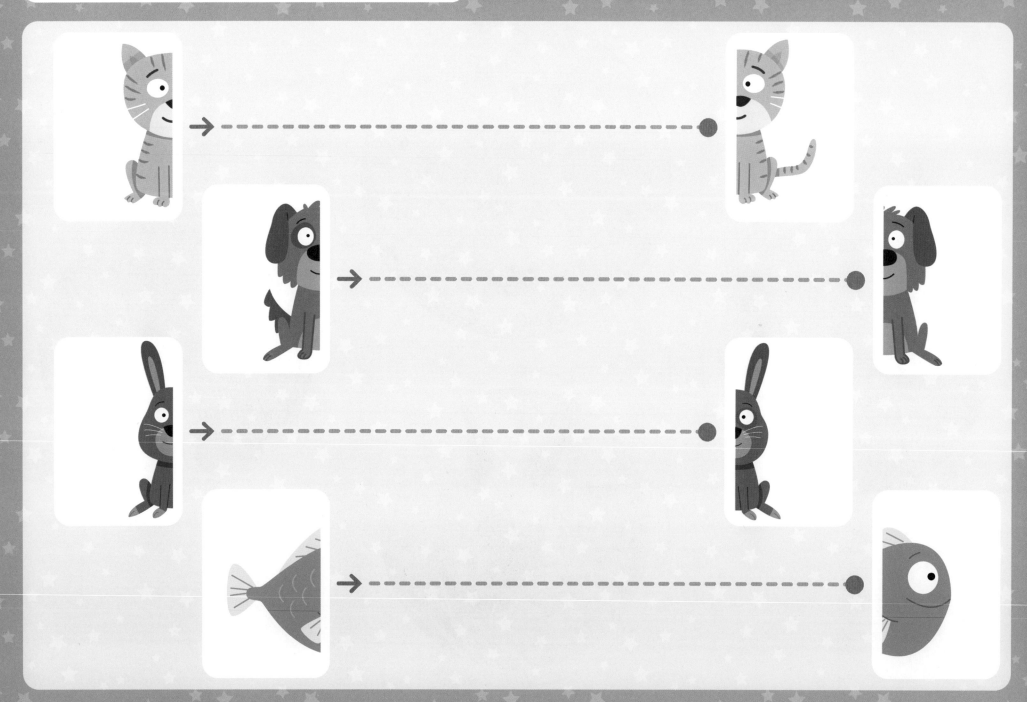

6 *cat, dog, rabbit, fish*

Look. **Make.** **Say.**

52 Listen. Find. Point. Say.

👁 Look. ✋ Count. ✏ Color.

5 6

7 8

6 8

5 7

7 Clothes

🎧 54 Listen. 👆 Point. ✏️ Color.

Put on your jacket.

🎧 55 Listen. ⬭ Stick. 👆 Point. 💬 Say.

7 Language practice: *(Put on / Take off) your (jacket / hat / socks / shoes).*

56 **Listen.** **Trace.** **Color.** **Say.**

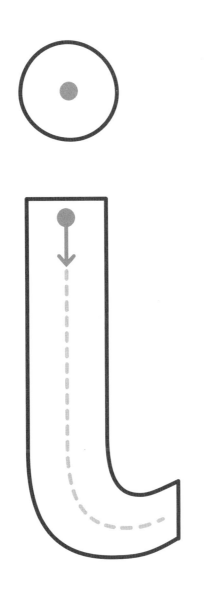

Listen. Tommy's T-shirt 🎧 57

I have a new dress.

7 **Language presentation:** *I have (a dress / pants / a T-shirt / a skirt).*

59 Listen. Color. Sing.

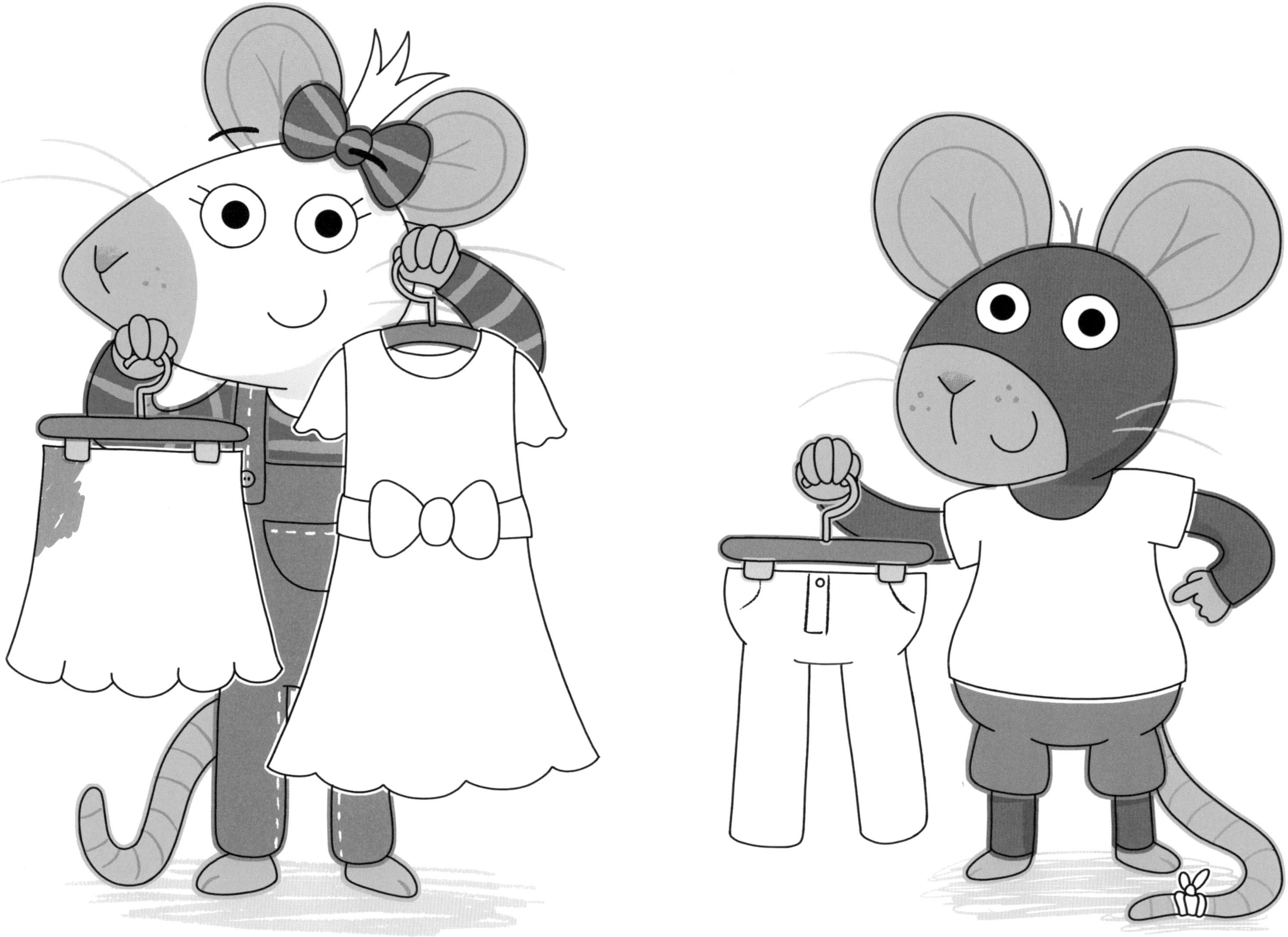

 **Look.** ✏ **Color.**

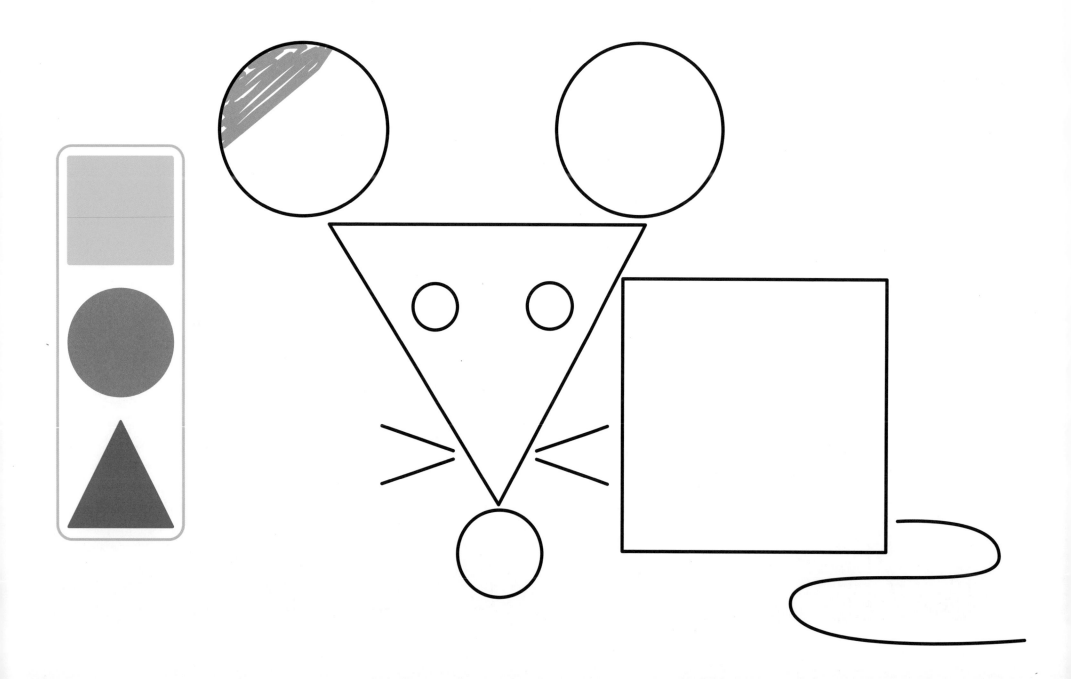

👁 Look. ⭕ Trace.

Look. **Listen.** **Match.** **Say.**

7 *I have (pants / a T-shirt / a jacket / socks / a dress / a hat / a skirt / shoes).*

Look.  Make. Say.

8 Transportation

🎧 63 Listen. ⬭ Stick. 👆 Point. 💬 Say.

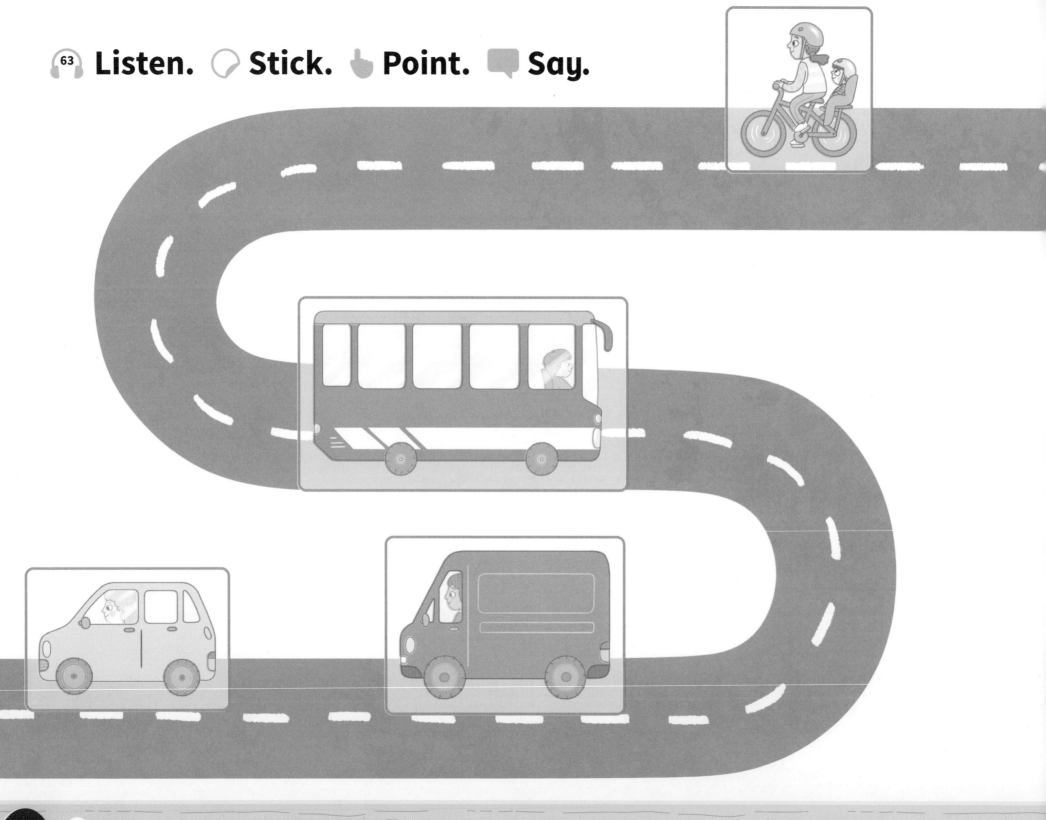

8 Language practice: *I can see a (car / van / bike / bus).*

🎧 64 **Listen.** ⭕ **Trace.** ✏️ **Color.** 💬 **Say.**

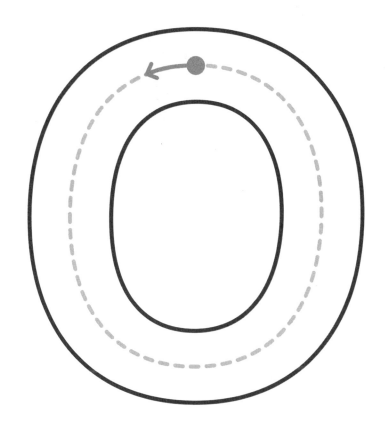

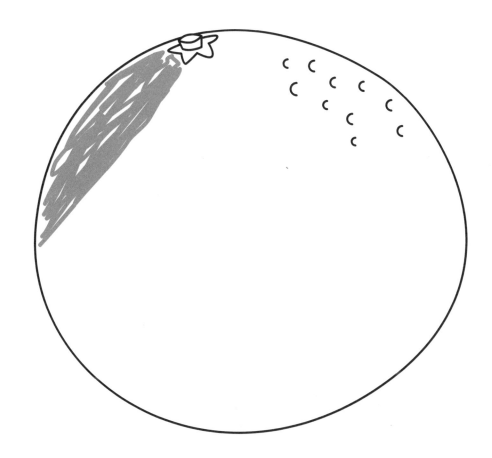

1

2

3

4

1

I can ride a bike.

2

3

4

▶ 🎧 **⁶⁷ Listen.** ◯ **Trace.** 🎵 **Sing.**

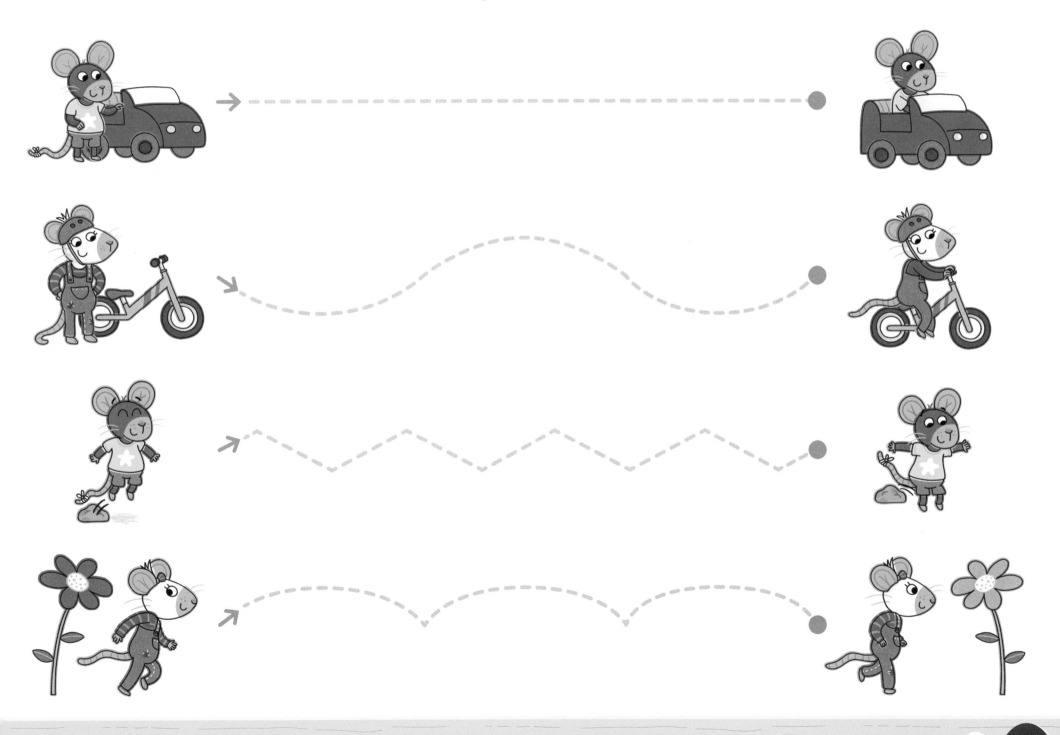

🎧 68 Listen. ✋ Count. ✏️ Color.

👁 **Look.** ✏ **Color.**

Look. Listen. Find. Circle. Say.

8 *I can see a (car / van / bike / bus).*

Look. Make. Play.

⑨ The park

▶ 🎧⁷⁰ **Listen to the song.**

🎧 72 Listen. ⬭ Stick. 👆 Point. 💬 Say.

9 **Language practice:** *a brown frog, a pink flower, a green tree, a blue bird*

73 **Listen.** ◯ **Trace.** ✏ **Color.** 💬 **Say.**

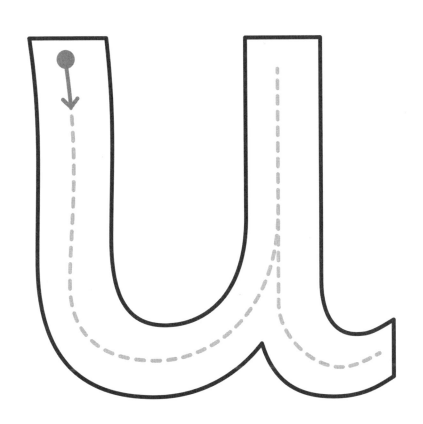

▶️ 🎧(74) Listen. Penny in the park

1

2

They're caterpillars.

3

4

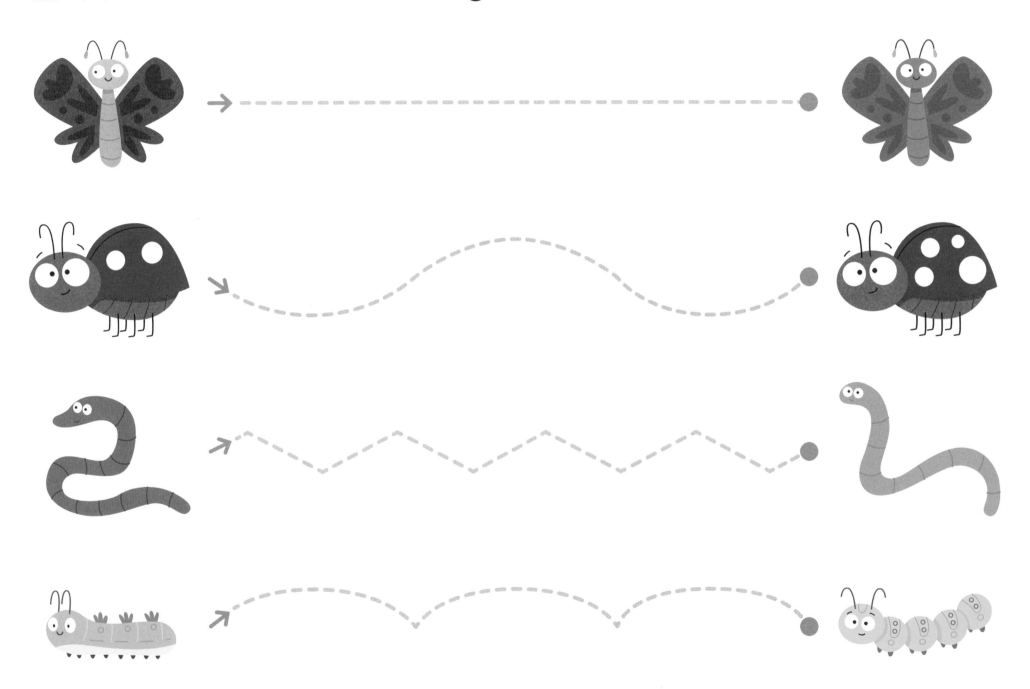

🎧 **77** **Listen.** ✋ **Count.** ✏️ **Color.**

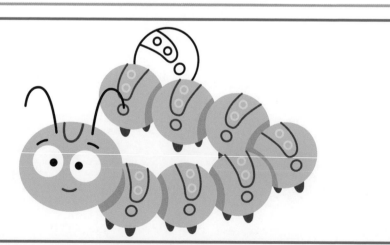

👁 **Look.** ✏ **Color.**

Follow. **Color.** **Say.**

9 *a pink worm, a green frog, a yellow caterpillar, a blue bird*

Look. Make. Say.

78 Listen. Find. Point. Say.

👁 **Look.** ✋ **Count.** ✏ **Color.**

3 **4** **5**

6 **8** **9**

7 **8** **10**

7 **9** **10**

Thanks and Acknowledgements

Authors' thanks

Many thanks to everyone at Cambridge University Press for their dedication and hard work in extraordinarily complicated circumstances, and in particular to:

Liane Grainger for her unwavering professionalism and her irrepressible joviality;

Emily Hird for her endless enthusiasm, good humor and sound judgement;

Jane Holt for her unflagging energy and her ability to bring the whole, sprawling project together;

Vanessa Gold for her hard work and sound editorial contribution.

Catherine Ball, Stephanie Howard and Carolyn Wright for their hard work helping to review, correct and knead the manuscript into shape.

Our thoughts and hearts go out to all the teachers and their students who have suffered and continue to suffer the devastating effects of the global pandemic that has changed all our lives. Stay strong.

Dedications

For my darling "ladies," Lydia and Silvia, with much love – CN

For Paloma, Pablo and Carlota, keep on smiling, love – MT

Caroline Nixon and Michael Tomlinson, Murcia, Spain

The publishers and authors would like to thank the following contributors:

Additional writing by Lesley Koustaff, Susan Rivers and Catherine Ball.

Book design and page make-up by Blooberry Design.

Cover design by Blooberry Design.

Commissioned photography by Blooberry Design.

Freelance editing by Catherine Ball, Karen Cleveland Marwick, Stephanie Howard and Carolyn Wright.

Editorial project management by Emma Ramírez.

Audio recording and production by Ian Harker.

Original songs and chants by Robert Lee.

Songs and chants production by Jake Carter.

Animation production by QBS and Collaborate Agency.

The authors and publishers acknowledge the following sources of copyright material and are grateful for the permissions granted. While every effort has been made, it has not always been possible to identify the sources of all the material used, or to trace all copyright holders. If any omissions are brought to our notice, we will be happy to include the appropriate acknowledgements on reprinting and in the next update to the digital edition, as applicable.

Key: U = Unit.

Photography

The following photos are sourced from Getty Images.

U1: Asya_mix/iStock/Getty Images Plus; Ariel Skelley/DigitalVision; kali9/E+; vbel71/iStock/Getty Images Plus; Jose Luis Pelaez Inc/DigitalVision; Dr T J Martin/Moment; milanvirijevic/E+; Jim Craigmyle/Stone; lisegagne/E+; Aleksandr Zubkov/Moment; studiocasper/E+; Danila Bolshakov/EyeEm; Irina_Strelnikova/iStock/Getty Images Plus; Lubushka/iStock/Getty Images Plus; Mai Vu/iStock/Getty Images Plus; antadi1332/iStock/Getty Images Plus; **U2:** Asya_mix/iStock/Getty Images Plus; eli_asenova/E+; FatCamera/E+; Maskot/DigitalVision; Shinya Sasaki/MottoPet; jezdicek; Sheila Jolley/The Image Bank; rimglow/iStock/Getty Images Plus; MahirAtes/iStock/Getty Images Plus; Nialif Surong/EyeEm; Bill Sykes/Cultura; SimonSkafar/E+; Julio Ricco/iStock/Getty Images Plus; Irina_Strelnikova/iStock/Getty Images Plus; Lubushka/iStock/Getty Images Plus; Mai Vu/iStock/Getty Images Plus; antadi1332/iStock/Getty Images Plus; **U3:** ivanastar/E+; Asya_mix/iStock/Getty Images Plus; SDI Productions/E+; DmitriMaruta/iStock/Getty Images Plus; Rastko Belic/EyeEm; Moussa81/iStock/Getty Images Plus; Stockbyte; Floortje/E+; Tobias Schwarz/iStock/Getty Images Plus; FuzzMartin/iStock/Getty Images Plus; Dan Thornberg/EyeEm; Chillim/iStock/Getty Images Plus; Irina_Strelnikova/iStock/Getty Images Plus; Lubushka/iStock/Getty Images Plus; Mai Vu/iStock/Getty Images Plus; antadi1332/iStock/Getty Images Plus; **U4:** Imgorthand/E+; Koichi Saito/a.collectionRF; Asya_mix/iStock/Getty Images Plus; Donald Iain Smith/Moment; Deborah Faulkner/Moment; Alexandra Grablewski/DigitalVision; MsMoloko/iStock/Getty Images Plus; Lubushka/iStock/Getty Images Plus; Mai Vu/iStock/Getty Images Plus; antadi1332/iStock/Getty Images Plus; **U5:** ArtMarie/E+; Asya_mix/iStock/Getty Images Plus; Peter Dazeley/The Image Bank; BJI/Blue Jean Images; Sudipta Haldar; Pineapple Studio/iStock/Getty Images Plus; Atw Photography/Photolibrary; Caziopeia/E+; fumumpa/E+;t_kimura/E+; imagestock/E+; IvonneW/iStock/Getty Images Plus; Spauln/E+; Jiraporn Gurle/EyeEm; GrashAlex/iStock/Getty Images Plus; Kwanchai Chai-Udom/EyeEm; rimglow/iStock/Getty Images Plus; jun xu/Moment; Nattawut Lakjit/EyeEm; Irina_Strelnikova/iStock/Getty Images Plus; Lubushka/iStock/Getty Images Plus; Mai Vu/iStock/Getty Images Plus; antadi1332/iStock/Getty Images Plus; **U6:** Fotosearch; Randy Faris/The Image Bank; Philip Thompson/EyeEm; Andrew_Howe/E+; Asya_mix/iStock/Getty Images Plus; Steven Greenfield/500px; Jose A. Bernat Bacete/Moment; Vincent Jacquesson/EyeEm; Irina_Strelnikova/iStock/Getty Images Plus; Lubushka/iStock/Getty Images Plus; Mai Vu/iStock/Getty Images Plus; antadi1332/iStock/Getty Images Plus; **U7:** Maskot; Peter Cade/Stone; Tara Moore/Stone; PhotoAlto/Jerome Gorin/PhotoAlto Agency RF Collections; Foodcollection GesmbH; bergamont/iStock/Getty Images Plus; Gazimal/The Image Bank; Asya_mix/iStock/Getty Images Plus; Irina_Strelnikova/iStock/Getty Images Plus; Lubushka/iStock/Getty Images Plus; Mai Vu/iStock/Getty Images Plus; antadi1332/iStock/Getty Images Plus; **U8:** Cavan Images; csheezio/E+; Virginia Star/Moment; triloks/E+; mevans/E+; John Lee; Johner Images; MsMoloko/iStock/Getty Images Plus; Asya_mix/iStock/Getty Images Plus; Lubushka/iStock/Getty Images Plus; Mai Vu/iStock/Getty Images Plus; antadi1332/iStock/Getty Images Plus; **U9:** HKPNC/E+; twomeows/Moment; Mike Bons/500px; Onfokus/E+; Floortje/iStock/Getty Images Plus; chictype/iStock/Getty Images Plus; MsMoloko/iStock/Getty Images Plus; Asya_mix/iStock/Getty Images Plus; Lubushka/iStock/Getty Images Plus; Mai Vu/iStock/Getty Images Plus; antadi1332/iStock/Getty Images Plus; Narongsak Kumma/EyeEm.

The following photo is sourced from another library.

U3: Oleksiy Mark/Shutterstock.

Illustrations

Amy Zhing; Beatriz Castro; Begoña Corbalán; Dean Gray; Louise Farshaw and Collaborate artists.

Cover illustration by Collaborate Agency.

1 My friends (Page 8)

2 My family (Page 20)

3 My toys (Page 32)

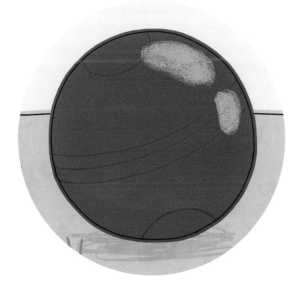

3 My toys (Page 32)

4 My body (Page 46)

5 Food (Page 58)

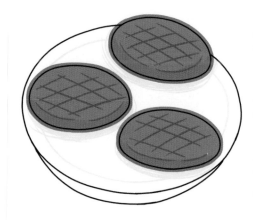
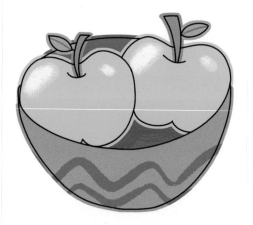

6 Animals (Page 70)

7 Clothes (Page 84)

8 Transportation (Page 96)

9 The park (Page 108)